WOMEN
AND FEMINISM
TODAY

BY CRYSTAL SANDS

ReferencePoint
Press®

San Diego, CA

LIBRARY OF CONGRESS CATALOGING-IN-PUBLICATION DATA

Name: Sands, Crystal, 1975– author.
Title: Women and Feminism Today/by Crystal Sands.
Description: San Diego, CA: ReferencePoint Press, Inc., [2019] | Series: Women and Society
| Audience: Grade 9 to 12 | Includes bibliographical references and index.
ISBN: 978-1-68282-547-1 (hardback)
ISBN: 978-1-68282-548-8 (ebook)
The complete Library of Congress record is available at www.loc.gov.

CONTENTS

IMPORTANT EVENTS IN
WOMEN'S HISTORY

1851
Sojourner Truth delivers her "Ain't I a Woman?" speech at the Ohio Women's Rights Convention.

1848
The Seneca Falls Convention is the first event held to discuss women's rights.

1872
Women's rights activist Susan B. Anthony is arrested for trying to vote.

1800	1825	1850	1875	1900

1776
Abigail Adams pleads with her husband, John Adams, to "remember the ladies" when forming the United States government.

1921
The American Birth Control League is founded by Margaret Sanger.

1869
The Wyoming territory grants women the right to vote.

1920
The United States passes the Nineteenth Amendment, granting women the right to vote.

MR. PRESIDENT WHAT WILL YOU DO FOR WOMAN SUFFRAGE

4

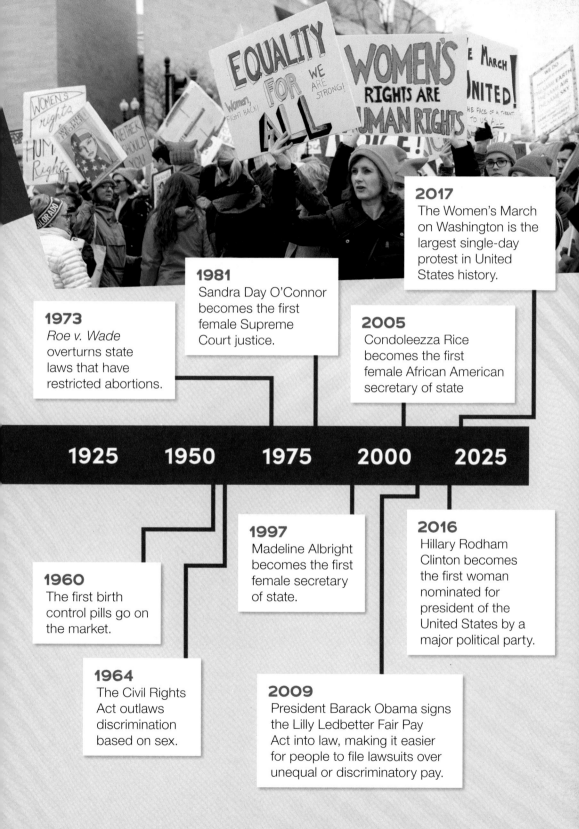

2017
The Women's March on Washington is the largest single-day protest in United States history.

1981
Sandra Day O'Connor becomes the first female Supreme Court justice.

1973
Roe v. Wade overturns state laws that have restricted abortions.

2005
Condoleezza Rice becomes the first female African American secretary of state

1925   1950   1975   2000   2025

1997
Madeline Albright becomes the first female secretary of state.

2016
Hillary Rodham Clinton becomes the first woman nominated for president of the United States by a major political party.

1960
The first birth control pills go on the market.

1964
The Civil Rights Act outlaws discrimination based on sex.

2009
President Barack Obama signs the Lilly Ledbetter Fair Pay Act into law, making it easier for people to file lawsuits over unequal or discriminatory pay.

FEMINISM TODAY

Feminism can be considered a controversial term in American culture today, and there are many disagreements about what feminism actually means. While some detractors associate feminism with women who hate men or who are angry at men, feminism is, at its core, about gender equality and fair treatment of women in a society that has historically favored men. For example, feminists argue for equal pay for equal work, as women generally make less money than men in the United States, even when both are working the same jobs.

In her book *We Should All Be Feminists*, Chimamanda Ngozi Adichie writes about her experiences as a feminist and discusses the stereotypes surrounding the word *feminist*. Other people defined feminism for Adichie in a way that she disagreed with. She was told she could not be a feminist because she was African, and feminists were white. She was told she could not be a feminist because she liked men, and feminists did not like men. She was told she could not be a feminist because she was not angry at men, and feminists were angry at men. In the end of her book, Adichie provides a powerful definition of feminism that is upheld by many modern activists: "My own definition of a feminist is a man or a woman who says, 'Yes, there's a problem with gender as it is today and we must fix it, we must do better.'"[1]

Many people who believe in gender equality do not want to be labeled feminists. A 2015 poll shows that while 85 percent of Americans believe in equality for women, only 18 percent consider themselves feminists. However, regardless of the label, it's clear that women's rights is an issue that many people care about. The Women's March on Washington on January 21, 2017, is estimated to be the largest single-day protest in United States history, with at least 4 million participants across the country. Sister marches took place around the world on that day.

FEMINIST ISSUES

Feminism in the United States has a long, rich history with roots stretching back to before the 1850s. It is through feminist movements that women obtained the right to vote in 1920, the right to hold public offices, and the right to work, among other achievements. But many people today realize that more work still needs to be done in order to obtain gender equality in American culture.

According to the Institute for Women's Policy Research, women make up almost half of the American workforce. Women are earning more college degrees than men, yet they continue to make less money than men. According to a 2016 study, full-time female workers on average made approximately eighty cents for every dollar that male workers earned. This is a gender pay gap of approximately 20 percent. The pay gap is worse for women of color, with black women earning just

The Women's March on Washington on January 21, 2017, was the largest single-day protest recorded in United States history. Women across the country and across the world marched in support of equal human rights.

sixty-three cents for every dollar a man earns. A Latina woman earns just fifty-four cents on the dollar compared with men. Research shows this pay gap remained stable from 2001 to 2016, with women making little progress. Additionally, according to a 2017 survey, approximately four in

ten women in the workforce
say they have experienced
gender discrimination at
work. This discrimination can
take many forms, such as
harassment and being passed
over for promotions, but the
most commonly reported
discrimination was unequal pay.

> "There are many women who do experience discrimination and abuse because of their gender as well as other parts of their identity."[2]
> —*Julia Bluhm, writer*

Women are also not equally represented in government positions in the United States. This unequal representation is considered especially problematic when government leaders make decisions on issues that largely affect women, such as reproductive health care. Additionally, women are not equally represented in business leadership roles.

One out of six women in the United States has been a victim of a rape or attempted rape. And out of every 1,000 rapes, 994 of the accused rapists will not be convicted of a crime, according to the Rape, Abuse, and Incest National Network (RAINN). That statistic includes unreported rapes, as most sexual violence is not reported to police. And according to a 2011 publication by the United Nations, 83 percent of girls in the United States experience some kind of sexual harassment at school.

These issues represent some of the continued struggles that feminists focus on in their activism and writing. Writer Julia Bluhm says, "There are many women who do experience discrimination and abuse because of their gender as well as other parts of their identity."[2] Feminism remains a part of American culture as women across the country continue to face inequality and discrimination.

CHAPTER ONE

WHAT IS THE HISTORY BEHIND FEMINISM?

Many think feminism may have started with the development of patriarchal society. In a patriarchal society, men are in positions of power. The roots of patriarchal society go back thousands of years or more. Throughout history, the United States has largely been patriarchal. But in recent history, women began to organize and fight against this structure.

CONQUEST, CAPITALISM, AND WOMEN

While the oppression of women is not universal, it is widespread in many cultures. Scholars and anthropologists today often point to the development of capitalism and specific religions as playing a vital role in this oppression. Scholars today point out that as capitalism developed, everything in nature became a commodity to men in power—and that included women. Women were seen as a resource to take advantage of. Authors Raj Patel and Jason Moore write:

First taking shape in the era of Christopher Columbus, capitalism created a peculiar binary order. "Nature" became the antonym of

Some elements of patriarchal society have ties to major world religions, such as Christianity. In Christianity, it is believed that the first woman on Earth, Eve, committed the original sin by disobeying God, which led to the downfall of all humans.

"society" in the minds of philosophers, in the policies of European empires, and the calculations of global financial centres. "Nature" was a place of profit, a vast frontier of free gifts waiting to be accepted by conquerors and capitalists. . . . In the centuries between Columbus and the industrial revolution, enslaved and indentured Africans, Asians, indigenous peoples and virtually all women became part of "nature"— and treated cheaply as a result.[3]

RELIGION AND WOMEN'S ROLES

Capitalism was not the only aspect of Western society that was oppressive to women. Religion and capitalism were closely connected in Western cultures. Christianity is one of several major world religions that has elements that can be considered oppressive to women, and it played an important role in women's lives in Europe and in the early American colonies. That role was, sometimes, not a good one. For example, in seventeenth-century Europe and the American colonies, many women were persecuted and killed as witches. These women were most often people who did not conform in their society or the church in some way. They could be easily blamed when anything unfortunate occurred, such as illness or famine. In her book *Hidden from History: 300 Years of Women's Oppression and the Fight Against It*, Sheila Rowbotham writes, "Many of the women who were accused of being witches were old and poor. Disputes arose between neighbours and when misfortunes came people looked for someone to blame. Old women who argued back were obvious targets."[4]

Christianity holds the belief that women were the creators of original sin. This idea developed from the story of Adam and Eve, the first man and woman on Earth. In this story, Eve was the one who was first tricked by the Devil in the Garden of Eden and the one who, therefore, brought forth the fall of mankind. This kind of religious story presents challenges for women that have been difficult to overcome. Christopher Witcombe, author and art history professor at Sweet Briar College, writes:

The story of Adam and Eve . . . is nonetheless perceived as containing fundamental, and largely negative, "truths" about the nature of women. . . . Eve represents everything about a woman a man should guard against. In both form and symbol, Eve is woman, and because of her, the prevalent belief in the West has been that all women are by nature disobedient, guileless, weak-willed, prone to temptation and evil, disloyal, untrustworthy, deceitful, seductive, and motivated in their thoughts and behavior purely by self-interest.[5]

As America was developing as a nation, women were active in churches and were considered to be important parts of religious society and culture. However, depictions of women in Christianity also contributed to the oppression of women at a societal level and in the home. Not only did women in America have no rights to property, they had no rights to their own children. According to Christianity, when a woman married, she became the property of her husband. This religious tradition was a part of common law (the general law of society) in early America. According to feminist scholar Sally Roesch Wagner, "This canon (church) law had been turned into common law, according to which married women were legally dead; therefore married women could not have custody of their children or rights to their own property or earnings, sign contracts, sue or be sued, or vote."[6] While many women found solace, peace, and purpose in their religion on a personal level, at a broader level, their religion was a part of their own oppression.

> "According to [common law], married women were legally dead; therefore married women could not have custody of their children or rights to their own property or earnings, sign contracts, sue or be sued, or vote."[6]
> —*Sally Roesch Wagner, feminist scholar*

WOMEN'S ROLES IN THE FAMILY

Life was difficult for women of many social classes and cultures in early America due to their lack of rights. Yet some women could find power in the work they performed at home, running their households. As the Industrial Revolution began to take hold in the United States and the country moved away from being a farming culture to a culture focused on factory work, more men began working outside of the home. While some women had jobs as well, the vast majority of work outside the home was completed by men. This left women in charge of running households and raising children. They handled a wide variety of work at very long hours. Una Robertson, author of *The Illustrated History of the Housewife*, writes that during the eighteenth and nineteenth centuries, a middle-class housewife's skills would have included, "healing the sick, cookery and the finer confectionary work, organizing great feasts . . . spinning of wool, linen, and hemp, and the subsequent making and dyeing of cloth."[7] Women would also be in charge of brewing, baking, cleaning, and a wide variety of other chores. Many argue that the work of these women facilitated the Industrial Revolution and the United States' subsequent development into one of the world's largest economies.

However, in some ways and for some women, the institution of marriage represented captivity. In cases of abuse, women usually had no options. They were stuck with abusive husbands. According to Roesch Wagner, "Until women's rights advocates began to change divorce laws in the last half of the nineteenth century, divorce was not allowed by church or state. Women fleeing from a violent husband could be returned to him by the police."[8]

Discussions of women's roles in early America often center around white women. But for black women, life generally was much harder. Almost all black women were slaves and had no say in any aspect of their lives. Their children were often taken from them. So, while white women were the first to begin speaking out for more rights both inside and outside the home, it is only because they were the ones with the freedom to do so. As the women's rights movement would take off in the late nineteenth century, for a time, women's rights and the issue of slavery were closely connected, with suffragists and abolitionists working side by side.

SOJOURNER TRUTH

Sojourner Truth was born enslaved in 1797. After gaining her freedom, she was a devoted abolitionist and women's rights activist. In 1851, she gave her most famous speech, "Ain't I a Woman?" at the Ohio Women's Rights Convention. Her speech was improvised but would become one of the most memorable speeches of the women's rights movement. In abolitionist circles, she was considered a radical because she wanted the abolitionist movement to seek civil rights for black women when the movement was primarily focused on rights for black men. Truth lived a harsh life while she was enslaved and eventually escaped to freedom in 1826. When the state of New York abolished slavery later in 1827, Truth's son was illegally sold to slaveholders in the South. Truth took this issue to court, and her son was returned from the South. She was the first black woman to successfully challenge a white man in court. Truth published her memoir, *The Narrative of Sojourner Truth: A Northern Slave*, in 1850. Today, she is remembered as an important leader in the abolitionist and women's rights movements.

A NEED FOR FEMINISM IN AMERICA

Even before the first official feminist movement in America during the nineteenth century, women were seeking equal rights and writing about it. Decades before women would organize and demand the right to vote, Abigail Adams, the wife of Founding Father John Adams, urged her husband to "remember the ladies." In a famous letter to her husband as he worked with the First Continental Congress to form the first government of the United States, she wrote:

> *I desire you would Remember the Ladies, and be more generous and favourable to them than your ancestors. Do not put such unlimited power into the hands of the Husbands. Remember all Men would be tyrants if they could. If perticuliar care and attention is not paid to the Laidies we are determined to foment a Rebelion, and will not hold ourselves bound by any Laws in which we have no voice, or Representation.*[9]

Abigail Adams, wife of American Founding Father John Adams, wrote one of the earliest documents calling for equal rights for women in the United States. In a letter to her husband, she asked him to "remember the ladies" while creating the country's laws.

Although women were excluded from many basic rights during the formation of the new American government, Adams's letter reveals that the issue of women's rights was on some women's minds. While the conditions in which women lived varied greatly in early America depending upon their race and the colony in which they lived, in general, women had little to no rights and were seen very much as property of their fathers and their husbands. Women were expected to be subservient and had little to no power. Most women were allowed little education, only enough to allow them to read the Bible. They were given no voice in the formation of the new United States. Even the goods they created as a part of their homemaking were the property of their husbands. The founding documents of the United States dedicated the new nation to the concepts of liberty and freedom. Yet the roles of women would change very little from what they had been in Europe, and it would be more than 100 years before women's rights would even be considered by those in power at the national level.

NATIVE AMERICAN CULTURES AND AMERICAN FEMINISM

How did feminists in the United States first learn that the conditions in which they lived in were not universal to all women? Some scholars point to the strong roles that Native American women had within their own cultures as a catalyst for some early aspects of the women's rights movement. It is documented that leaders of the women's rights movement had close connections to Iroquois leaders, both men and women. In Iroquois culture, women were not perceived as property in the same way that European women were. In the absence of capitalism and Christianity, Iroquois women were often leaders in their communities and had equal rights in their marriages. Leaders of the feminist movement during the nineteenth century were close with Iroquois women, and scholars now assert that because of this, white women started to better understand that the oppression they experienced was not universal in all human cultures.

EARLY AMERICAN FEMINISTS

Abigail Adams was not the only woman to speak for women's rights. Women in the mid-nineteenth century were writing about their rights

In the 1800s and 1900s, women started to get jobs outside the home, including in factories. This offered them some independence, but they were still not considered equal to men.

and the need for gender equality in America, setting the stage for the First Wave of feminism, which would begin by the end of the nineteenth century. While America was defining itself as a country separate from England, some women argued that it was time for America to define a better life for women. Women were still not educated in the same ways men were, and they had few rights in terms of property ownership. They were still expected to be subservient to men, even though during the nineteenth century women began to get jobs and work outside the home.

As America was shifting from an agricultural economy to an industrial economy in the nineteenth century, some women went to work in factories. According to archivists for the Baker Library of Harvard Business School:

> Women made up a large segment of the new factory labor force, especially for the textile industry. In order to work in the new industrial towns, like Lowell and Lawrence, Massachusetts, young women moved away from their hometowns to live in factory boarding houses. The salaries they received, as well as the separation from their families, offered women a new type of financial and psychological independence.[10]

In 1836, the women textile workers were the first American laborers to go on strike for better working conditions. Women who had been working in the textile mills joined together in order to fight for better working conditions and higher pay.

Also during the nineteenth century, Margaret Fuller, an early American feminist, wrote about the need for a women's movement in America. She was a writer who worked with famous literary figures such as Ralph Waldo Emerson. Fuller helped Emerson develop a well-respected literary journal of the time period. She also wrote several important feminist works, including *Woman in the Nineteenth Century*, published in 1845. In this groundbreaking work, she wrote:

> It may be said that Man does not have his fair play either; his energies are repressed and distorted by the interposition of artificial obstacles. Ay, but he himself has put them there; they have grown out of his own imperfections. If there is a misfortune in Woman's lot, it is in obstacles being interposed by men, which do not mark her state; and, if they express her past ignorance, do not her present needs. As every Man is of Woman born, she has slow but sure means of redress; yet the sooner a general justness of thought makes smooth the path, the better.[11]

In this passage, Fuller makes it clear that men were also repressed in American culture. This point would come up again in the feminist movement in the coming centuries. But Fuller emphasizes that men created their own oppression, as they were in charge of society. She argues that women are up against obstacles of oppression that are not of their own making. She continues by pointing out that women will be able to make slow progress, but swifter fairness would be better.

The works of women such as Fuller would set the stage for a large, cohesive women's movement that would be coming soon to the United States. This movement would mark significant progress in the treatment of women and their place in American society. Up until the Seneca Falls Convention in 1848, women had been speaking out against oppression as individuals. But women eventually started to work together on a larger scale. Inspired by the abolitionist movement to end slavery in the United States, women began to organize for women's rights as well.

SENECA FALLS CONVENTION AND FIRST WAVE FEMINISM

In 1848, leaders of the feminist movement organized the first formal women's rights convention in the United States. Held in Seneca Falls, New York, the convention focused on drafting goals for the women's rights movement. There were more than 200 women in attendance. The meeting officially launched the women's suffrage movement, or the movement to fight for women's rights to vote. According to Jean Matthews, author of *Women's Struggle for Equality: The First Phase*, "Seneca Falls marked a qualitative step forward in the

"Seneca Falls marked a qualitative step forward in the evolution of the Woman Question. . . . A group of women were organizing as a collectivity and producing a statement that invited public assent."[12]
—*Jean Matthews, author of* Women's Struggle for Equality: The First Phase

The First Wave of feminism largely focused on women achieving the right to vote. Groups of women protested in parades and picket lines, like this one, for years until women were granted the right to vote in 1920.

evolution of the Woman Question. Earlier feminist statements had been the work of individuals, speaking and writing as individuals. Now a group of women were organizing as a collectivity and producing a statement that invited public assent."[12] The Seneca Falls Convention would set the stage for other conventions and more organized efforts for women's rights.

The key issues to emerge from the formal women's rights movement that developed after the Seneca Falls Convention were the right to vote, the right to own property, and the right for women to own themselves or their own bodies in marriage. These early feminists were calling for a new kind of equality in marriage, one that was revolutionary for the time.

ELIZABETH CADY STANTON AND LUCRETIA MOTT

The Seneca Falls Convention was organized by Elizabeth Cady Stanton and Lucretia Mott, abolitionists who met at the 1840 World Anti-Slavery Convention in London. Both women were banned from the anti-slavery convention's floor simply because they were women. After that, the two came together. In organizing the Seneca Falls Convention, Stanton and Mott helped found the women's rights movement in the United States. Two weeks after the Seneca Falls Convention, a larger convention was held in Rochester, New York. Similar women's rights conventions were held annually after that until the passage of the Nineteenth Amendment in 1920, which granted women the right to vote.

According to Matthews, "In marrying, women stepped into a realm of separate law where the protections they had hitherto enjoyed no longer applied. The wife gave up not only her right to control her property but the right to control her person. . . . In confronting the question of marital power, feminists were entering a real thicket. It was one thing to deprive a husband of rights over his wife's property, quite another to question his marital rights over her body."[13]

Lucy Stone was a prominent abolitionist and feminist during this period. She was the first woman from Massachusetts to earn a college degree. In an 1856 letter to Antoinette Brown Blackwell, the first woman to be ordained as a Protestant minister in the United States, Stone wrote:

It is clear to me that the [marriage] question underlies this whole movement and all our little skirmishing for better laws and the right to vote, will yet be swallowed up, in the real question, viz, has woman, as wife, a right to herself? It is very little to me, to have the right to vote, to own property, etc, if I may not keep my body, and its uses, in my absolute right. Not one wife in a thousand can do that right now, & so long as she suffers this bondage, all other rights will not help her to her true position.[14]

Strong feminist leaders began to emerge in the late nineteenth and early twentieth century. These women would be the founders of a movement that would later be referred to as the First Wave of the feminist movement. Outspoken women such as Susan B. Anthony became known as important leaders in the movement. These women who were working for women's rights during the mid-nineteenth century would become icons of feminism that remain admired today. Anthony worked tirelessly for women's voting rights, giving speeches all over the country.

Before 1920, women could not vote in federal elections. The First Wave of feminism made voting rights a top priority. Feminist leaders, such as Anthony, wrote, lobbied, and protested for the right to vote. Elizabeth Cady Stanton, one of the leaders of the Seneca Falls Convention, ran for Congress in 1866, receiving only 24 votes. Anthony illegally voted in the 1872 election. She was arrested and was not allowed to testify on her own behalf in court. Years later, in the 1910s, Alice Paul organized parades and picket lines fighting for women's right to vote. Like Anthony, Paul was arrested for her protests. Paul and nearly 200 women protesters spent months in jail in 1917. Anthony and Stanton both died before women were granted the right to vote. But their work for women's rights helped bring about the Nineteenth Amendment to the Constitution on August 18, 1920. Finally, American women could vote.

SECOND WAVE FEMINISM

Between 1967 and 1969, a new generation of feminists would take center stage. Inspired by and connected to the civil rights movement and the protests against the Vietnam War (1954–1975), this movement came to be called the Women's Liberation Movement. Two key issues to emerge during this period were the right to work and reproductive rights. Shortly after World War II (1939–1945), during which women had gone to work in record numbers in the United States, social movements of the 1960s would inspire a new generation of feminists. And, while many modern feminists perceive that the Second Wave focused on issues for middle-class white women, the movement's roots were in women who had fought for civil rights and for an end to the Vietnam War.

Margaret Sanger was a leader in the movement to legalize birth control and make it readily available for women in the United States. She was one of eleven children and saw her fifty-year-old mother die from tuberculosis after enduring the stress of eleven childbirths and seven miscarriages. Sanger became a nurse and opened the first birth control clinic in the United States. She eventually founded what is known today as Planned Parenthood, an organization that remains an advocate for reproductive rights, abortion rights, and women's health care. Sanger had been involved in caring for women who had resorted to illegal abortions. Caring for women who had been given botched abortions and seeing these women's trauma and suffering inspired Sanger to advocate for better birth control. Sanger wrote, "No woman can call herself free who does not own and control her body. No woman can call herself free until she can choose consciously whether she will or will not be a mother."[15]

"No woman can call herself free who does not own and control her body. No woman can call herself free until she can choose consciously whether she will or will not be a mother."[15]
—Margaret Sanger, Second Wave feminism leader

Although her work was controversial, Sanger helped develop oral contraceptives, or the birth control pill, which was approved by the Food and Drug Administration (FDA) in 1960. The pill has improved the lives of women throughout the world by giving women some control over when they have children, an issue critical to the Second Wave of feminism. According to the Guttmacher Institute, a leading research institute of public policy in the United States, women are able to use birth control to maintain a healthier space between pregnancies and to avoid pregnancies too early or too late in life, when health risks are higher for both women and their babies. The ability to delay children is also crucial to women's social and economic advancement.

But the Second Wave of feminism was about more than birth control. Second Wave feminists fought for equal rights in the workplace, though discrimination would continue. They raised awareness about the objectification of women through protests, including a protest of the Miss America Pageant in 1968, which was attended by approximately 400 feminists. At its peak, the majority of women in the United States identified with the Second Wave movement. The work of feminists from the 1960s to the 1980s set the stage for the modern movements of feminism today.

CHAPTER TWO
WHAT DOES MODERN FEMINISM LOOK LIKE?

IIII

The fight for equality and women's rights was not over after the Second Wave of feminism. The Third Wave of feminism, which began in the 1990s, blended into the Fourth Wave of feminism, which continues in the twenty-first century and is still evolving. Feminism today adjusts to events in American culture. Many credit the beginning of the Third Wave of feminism to an article published in *Ms.* magazine by then twenty-two-year-old Rebecca Walker. In the 1990s, during confirmation hearings for Supreme Court Justice Clarence Thomas, Thomas was accused of sexual harassment in the workplace. His accuser, Anita Hill, testified before Congress with details of the alleged harassment. When Thomas was confirmed to the Supreme Court, many women were upset and argued that the allegations against him were not taken seriously by Congress.

At that time, Walker penned an essay that inspired women to organize. She wrote, "So I write this plea to all women, especially the women of my generation: Let Thomas' confirmation serve to remind you,

MS. MAGAZINE

Ms. magazine is a revolutionary American women's magazine first published in 1971 as an insert in *New York* magazine. It first appeared as a separate magazine in 1972 and was published in that format every month from 1972 to 1987. As of 2018, the magazine was still in print but was published on a quarterly basis. *Ms.* magazine was founded by Second Wave feminists Gloria Steinem and Dorothy Pitman Hughes. The magazine was meant to be a voice in the mainstream media for women that was actually created by women. The magazine's first years focused on challenging social norms for women. Steinem and Hughes wanted a magazine for women that would focus on topics beyond fashion and housekeeping. The magazine was originally going to be called *Sojourner*, named after Sojourner Truth, but this title was perceived as being the title of a travel magazine. Some important milestones in the feminist movement come from works published in *Ms.* The magazine made history when, in 1972, it published names of women who had had abortions. The Supreme Court would legalize abortion a year later. A story published in 1976 was the first story to address the issue of domestic violence in a national magazine.

as it did me, that the fight is far from over. Let this dismissal of a woman's experience move you to anger. Turn that outrage into political power. . . . I am not a postfeminist feminist. I am the Third Wave."[16]

THIRD WAVE FEMINISM

Building upon the successes of the First and Second Waves of feminism, Third Wave feminists worked to be even more inclusive, ensuring they were moving beyond experiences of only white, middle-class women. They began to explore ways in which the patriarchal structure in the United States was harmful to women of color, minority groups in general, and men. One important voice of Third Wave feminism was bell hooks,

"So I write this plea to all women, especially the women of my generation: Let [Clarence] Thomas' confirmation serve to remind you, as it did me, that the fight is far from over. Let this dismissal of a woman's experience move you to anger. Turn that outrage into political power. . . . I am not a postfeminist feminist. I am the Third Wave."[16]

—*Rebecca Walker, writer*

BELL HOOKS

Gloria Jean Watkins is better known by her pen name, bell hooks. She is an author, scholar, feminist, educator, and social activist. She has published more than thirty books and often writes about issues of race, gender, and capitalism. She was born in 1952 and grew up in racially segregated Kentucky. After high school, she went to Stanford University, earning her bachelor's degree there in 1973. She earned her doctorate in literature from the University of California, Santa Cruz in 1983. bell hooks began her teaching career as an English professor at the University of Southern California and published *Ain't I A Woman?: Black Women and Feminism* in 1981. Her 1984 work, *Feminist Theory: From Margin to the Center*, noted the lack of diversity in the most popular feminist theories. Her efforts have helped bring intersectionality to the women's movement in the United States and provided feminists with important perspective. She advocates for women to understand and accept their differences but to work together to fight against oppression. bell hooks also advocates that feminism must focus on helping all genders and must work with men to end oppression of people in a patriarchal capitalistic society.

a black woman. hooks, who prefers for her name to be lowercased, continues to write about feminism today, well into the Fourth Wave. In her work, she writes about the oppression of women and how the patriarchal system is oppressive not only to women but to many men as well. In her introduction to her 2014 book, *Feminism is for Everybody*, hooks argues that feminism benefits everyone and that equality for women benefits everyone. She takes feminism out of academia and relates it to everyday life for people. She explains that many men do not like being a part of a patriarchal system that oppresses women: "Most men are disturbed by hatred and fear of women, by male violence against women, even the men who perpetuate this violence. But they fear letting go of the benefits [of patriarchy]. They are

> "Most men are disturbed by hatred and fear of women, by male violence against women, even the men who perpetuate this violence. But they fear letting go of the benefits [of patriarchy]. They are not certain what will happen to the world they know most intimately if patriarchy changes."[17]
>
> —bell hooks, writer

not certain what will happen to the world they know most intimately if patriarchy changes."[17]

The ideas hooks asserts about how the patriarchy is oppressive to both men and women came to be better known and understood during the Third Wave of feminism, and the ideas continue to be an important part of feminism today. However, not all agree with hooks's approach to feminism, and there are branches of feminism that began during the Third Wave that continue into the Fourth Wave today. These branches of feminism present different theories about feminism, and the women involved have different goals.

BRANCHES OF MODERN FEMINISM

Some of the many branches of modern feminism include Marxist Feminism, Black Feminism, Ecofeminism, Radical Feminism, and Intersectional Feminism. Marxist Feminism aligns with the works of philosophers Karl Marx and Frederick Engels and focuses on the ways in which women are oppressed through capitalistic systems of money and private property. They argue that capitalism is a root cause of women's oppression.

Black Feminism is a branch of feminism that focuses on women of color, who face discrimination based on both race and gender. While some modern feminists think that this branch of feminism is a recent development, its history goes back to the eighteenth and nineteenth centuries. Black Feminists say that because women of color face discrimination based on both race and gender, they experience what some call the *double bind*. This double bind means that women of color are being oppressed in a variety of ways, and Black Feminists often argue that the traditional approaches to feminism have focused too much on the experiences of white women. According to the *Encyclopedia of African-American Culture and History*, Black Feminism has three key tenets:

First, that black men have often asserted their "rights to be men" by restricting these same rights for black women; second, that black male leaders often consider it inappropriate for black women to play a leading role in fighting for black freedom and justice; third, that mainstream feminism in the United States, from the suffragists to pro-choice advocates, define feminism by excluding the needs and rights of women of color and poor women.[18]

Ecofeminists see the oppression of women as closely connected to the oppression of nature. As men historically worked to conquer nature, women became a part of nature to be conquered. Ecofeminists speak up for women's rights and the rights of the planet. They fight against nuclear arms races, environmental destruction, and similar global problems.

Radical Feminism holds many of the same goals as other branches of feminism—equal rights for women, regardless of age, race, or social class. However, Radical Feminism differs in that it seeks spaces for women to learn, grow, and find power without men. Unlike some branches of feminism that seek to work within the patriarchal system to gain more rights for women, Radical Feminism argues for a complete dismantling of the system. According to scholars Susan M. Shaw and Janet Lee, authors of *Women's Voices, Feminist Visions*, "Radical feminists recognize the oppression of women as a fundamental political oppression wherein women are categorized as inferior based on their gender. It is not enough to remove obstacles; rather, deeper, more transformational changes need to be made in societal institutions (like the government or media) as well as in people's heads."[19]

Another important branch of modern feminism is Intersectional Feminism. Most modern feminists embrace Intersectional Feminism as a part of their stance. Intersectional Feminism specifically advocates for the equal rights for all women and understands that experiences related to gender, class, sexual orientation, ethnicity, culture, and religion all intersect

Many modern feminists want to broaden the movement to encompass all human rights causes. For example, Intersectional Feminism aims to consider the ways that gender, class, sexual orientation, and other characteristics intersect to create different experiences of oppression.

to form experiences of oppression. According to a 2017 article in *USA Today*, "'Intersectional Feminism' is much more than the latest feminist buzzword. It is a decades-old term many feminists use to explain how the feminist movement can be more diverse and inclusive."[20]

Ultimately, modern feminism is a movement that has lasted for decades. Some experts disagree on exactly what the differences are between Third Wave and Fourth Wave feminism. "The confusion surrounding what constitutes third wave feminism is in some respects its defining feature," says feminist scholar Elizabeth Evans.[21] And the Fourth Wave is still evolving. But overall, modern feminism often greatly emphasizes inclusivity, diversity, and the use of social media more than feminists of the past—to the extent that some people who could be classified as Fourth Wave feminists are not fully comfortable with the label *feminist*. Fourth Wave feminism tends to focus more on the oppression of all people under the patriarchal system, causing many members of that movement to want to use the label *humanist* instead of *feminist*. Still, Martha Rampton, director of the Center for Gender Equity at Pacific University, writes:

> *Some people who wish to ride this new fourth wave have trouble with the word "feminism," not just because of its older connotations of radicalism, but because the word feels like it is underpinned by assumptions of a gender binary and an exclusionary subtext: "for women only." Many fourth wavers who are completely on-board with the movement's [tenets] find the term "feminism" sticking in their craws and worry that it is hard to get their message out with a label that raises hackles for a broader audience. Yet the word is winning the day. The generation now coming of age sees that we face serious problems because of the way society genders and is gendered, and we need a strong "in-your-face" word to combat those problems. Feminism no longer just refers to the struggles of women; it is a clarion call for gender equity.[22]*

ISSUES FOR MODERN FEMINISM

The goals of all of the branches of modern feminism are similar in focus, and the issues they contend with affect all American women, making feminism still a relevant and important cause today. Despite progress that was made for women's rights in the First and Second Waves of feminism,

One issue of modern feminism is the lack of paid maternity leave in the United States. Many mothers struggle with deciding how much time they can afford to take off from work when they have a baby.

women's roles in the family and society remain difficult, and oppression remains an issue.

According to the US Department of Labor, nearly one in four new mothers goes back to work just two weeks after having a new baby.

Part of the reason for this is that the United States does not require employers to offer paid leave for new mothers. Eligible workers across the country get twelve weeks unpaid leave to care for a new child. However, not all families can afford to have a working mother go unpaid for twelve weeks. There are some companies that offer paid leave for new parents, but many do not. This is bad for the health of both women and their children. Emily Peck, a senior reporter for the *Huffington Post*, explained in a 2015 article, "A full-time waitress working more than 60 hours a week told Lerner [a reporter] that when her son was just 4 weeks old, she would come home exhausted and sleep with one hand on her baby because that's the only connection she could get."[23]

Issues related to women's portrayal in the media remain important as well. According to author Gayle Pitman, images of women in the media continue to have a powerful negative influence on other women and young girls. She writes, "Our culture is saturated with toxic media which sends powerful messages to girls and women about how to be beautiful, sexy, flawless, and desirable for others (particularly for boys and men)."[24] Pitman goes on to explain, "Studies have shown that girls and women who are regular readers of traditional women's magazines tend to feel more negatively about their bodies, compared to girls and women who don't read these magazines. . . . Even with the surge of Internet use, women's magazines continue to be popular."[25]

"Studies have shown that girls and women who are regular readers of traditional women's magazines tend to feel more negatively about their bodies, compared to girls and women who don't read these magazines."[25]
— *Gayle Pitman, writer*

Issues related to sexual harassment and gender discrimination at work remain serious problems for modern women. There is also a gender pay gap, meaning that on average, women make less money than men, even for the same work. Women are also underrepresented in many government and business leadership positions.

WOMEN'S MARCH ON WASHINGTON

The need for a strong, modern feminist movement could be seen with the 2017 Women's March on Washington. As the largest single-day protest in American history, the march was a landmark event that made people aware of how serious modern feminists were. The Women's March took place on January 21, 2017. Sister marches happened around the world that same day. The Women's March was organized to bring awareness to a variety of human rights issues, including women's rights, immigration reform, health care reform, environmental issues, racial inequality, and LGBTQIA (lesbian, gay, bisexual, transgender, queer or questioning, intersex, asexual) rights. Although the march was focused on these key issues, it also developed in opposition to President Donald Trump, who had been sworn in as president the day before the march. Trump has a history of making controversial and offensive comments about women and others, including while he was a presidential candidate. So, many Women's March protesters focused their attention on sending a strong message to the new president that women's rights and other human rights are important. It is estimated that between 3.2 million and 5.2 million people participated in the march in the United States. Worldwide, the total number reached more than 7 million. There were 408 marches in the United States and 168 in eighty-one other countries around the world, including Canada and Mexico. The protest reached every continent in the world. It is estimated that one in every 100 Americans attended a march. Activists Gloria Steinem, Angela Davis, Michael Moore, and Maryum Ali, along with actresses Scarlett Johansson, America Ferrera, and Ashley Judd were among the many famous speakers at the protest.

Organizers of the Women's March on Washington developed a website to provide a list of goals for their protests and to promote their

Actress America Ferrera was among several celebrities to speak at the 2017 Women's March on Washington. These activists called for women to come together to demand fair treatment and support human rights.

continued work for women's rights. They had a number of stated goals as a part of their overall mission: reproductive rights, LGBTQIA rights, workers' rights, civil rights, disability rights, immigrant rights, environmental justice, and ending violence. Because modern feminism seeks to end all kinds of oppression, it has broadened to encompass this wide variety of social justice issues, and the issues are often interconnected.

In an example on the issue of workers' rights, in June 2018 the Supreme Court ruled against workers' unions and found that union members do not have to pay dues to a union they disagree with politically. This was a huge blow to unions because the Supreme Court decision puts union funding at risk. While this may not seem like it would be an issue for feminism, the decision is considered to be a blow to women and people of color as well. According to the National Women's Law Center, women make up fifty-five percent of public sector union workers. Moreover, according to the Institute for Women's Policy Research, union jobs are particularly beneficial to Hispanic women. According to the data, Hispanic women who are union members earn an average of $820.00 per week for full-time work compared to the average of $565.00 per week for nonunion full-time work.

There are some feminists who contend that modern feminism is trying to address too much with its focus on so many human rights and environmental issues. In a 2017 essay for *The Nation*, feminist Katha Pollitt writes about her concerns that feminism is widening its focus too much and that the lack of focus may be detrimental to the movement. She writes:

We don't ask other progressive movements to take on so many tasks, let alone expand their briefs to include feminist issues. Environmentalists don't have to demand equal pay and affordable child care; labor movements aren't

"Perhaps the women's movement is simply more advanced and broad-based, and we are about to see a left led largely by feminist women. That would be fantastic. Or perhaps the women's movement is at risk of diffusing itself in too many directions."[26]
—*Katha Pollitt, feminist*

Modern feminists aim to address many issues. One is workers' rights, which includes making sure people are fairly compensated for their work.

expected to call for the abolition of rape culture . . . perhaps the women's movement is simply more advanced and broad-based, and we are about to see a left led largely by feminist women. That would be fantastic. Or perhaps the women's movement is at risk of diffusing itself in too many directions, and (as has happened many times in the history of the left) fighting the specific subordinations of women to men will be sidelined in the service of some supposedly larger goal.[26]

But while spreading itself too thin may be a serious issue modern feminism will have to contend with eventually, for now the movement still seems to be broadly focused on inclusivity and human suffering in general. According to the Women's March official website, its mission is to address "a diverse range of issues."[27] It is committed to "dismantling systems of oppression."[28] With such diverse and important goals, most agree that there is much work yet to do.

CHAPTER THREE

WHAT OBSTACLES DOES MODERN FEMINISM FACE?

Among the biggest obstacles that modern feminism faces are negative connotations of the word *feminist* and misperceptions or misrepresentations of feminists. Feminists are often negatively perceived as too outspoken or not gentle enough. Elizabeth Johnston writes about the historical portrayal of powerful women in her essay "The Original Nasty Woman," which was published in the *Atlantic* magazine days before the 2016 presidential election in the United States. In her essay, Johnston explores the connections between strong women and their portrayal as the Medusa figure from Greek mythology. Medusa was a powerful female monster, and the only way to kill her was to cut off her head. Johnston writes, "In Western culture, strong women have historically been imagined as threats requiring male conquest and control, and Medusa herself has long been the go-to figure for those seeking to demonize female authority."[29] Johnston goes on to provide a long list of strong, outspoken women in Western culture who have been portrayed in the media as the Medusa, including media mogul Oprah Winfrey; Condoleezza Rice, the first black woman to serve as US Secretary of State; Angela Merkel,

Greek mythology features Medusa, a female monster with snakes on her head. Scholars today trace negative stereotypes of powerful women back to mythical characters like Medusa.

chancellor of Germany; and politician Hillary Clinton, the first woman to be nominated for US president by a major political party.

PUBLIC PERCEPTION OF FEMINISM

Negative stereotypes, such as a Medusa figure, have historically been a challenge for feminists, and those stereotypes remain a challenge today. When Susan B. Anthony became a part of the American Anti-Slavery Society in 1856, she faced hostile mobs and armed threats. People threw things at her, and some hung her image in effigy. In a 2005 survey, 17 percent of women polled said that being called a feminist was considered an insult. There are even social media groups that aim to bring together women—mainly young women—who do not want to be considered feminists. Some people say these groups do not understand that the feminist movement is about pursuing gender equality. Others say that modern feminists need to address this backlash against the term *feminism* in order for the movement to continue making progress.

Many women speaking out against the term *feminism* feel that their experiences are not being fully represented in the modern feminist movement. It can be very difficult for all women, who each have different experiences, to unite under common goals. For example, many feel that organized modern feminism does not focus enough on the specific experiences of women of color. In her 2015 article "If We Divide, We Don't Conquer," feminist Carmen Rios writes, "If you're not a person of color, conversations about race might not come easy for you. It can be hard to relate to movements outside of our realm of experience."[30]

> "If you're not a person of color, conversations about race might not come easy for you. It can be hard to relate to movements outside of our realm of experience."[30]
> —*Carmen Rios, feminist writer*

Disagreements surrounding the term *feminism* present obstacles in the path toward a cohesive movement for women's rights and gender equality. Uniting the diverse experiences of all women remains one of feminism's biggest challenges. However, modern feminists are working to build on the work of feminists such as bell hooks to embrace a more intersectional view of feminism.

DIVERSITY OF EXPERIENCES

The feminist movement has historically focused on the plight of white, middle-class women. This is partly why some women find it difficult to identify with feminism. To some, feminism today still appears to be focused on white women, despite efforts within the movement to include people of all races and backgrounds.

Evidence of exclusion in modern feminism can be seen in some reactions to the historic Women's March in 2017. The march was attended by women from many different backgrounds. But some women of color would later express frustration about the many white women who attended the Women's March but had ignored previous protests that focused on racial injustices. Author S.T. Holloway described her frustration with that:

> [T]his deliberate ignorance fosters a culture where millions protest when white women's access to health care is threatened, but when black maternal death rates in the United States are on par with women in countries like Mexico and Uzbekistan, there is no national outrage or call for reform or worldwide protest. It is these issues affecting women of color, along with the effects of mass incarceration on our communities, the rate at which our children are disproportionately punished in schools, the lack of access to quality and affordable health care, the threat of destroying families as a result of deportation, the disproportionately high number of black trans women that are murdered, and so on, that are often met by deafening silence by our white sisters.[31]

As the one-year anniversary of the Women's March approached in 2018, national organizers of the march said they were working to address these concerns and to make the movement feel more inclusive. Thousands of women from different backgrounds marched again in 2018.

Differences in social class have also long been an obstacle in uniting women around feminist stances. But with the financial gap between rich and poor people growing with each passing year in the United States, the issue may be even more significant to modern feminism. In the 1970s,

Some people say modern feminism is not inclusive enough and continues to mostly focus on empowering white, middle- or upper-class women. Many feminists are working to address this concern.

feminist leader Kitty Ellickson had concerns about the new generation of feminists: "The younger generation of activists, born in prosperity and educated for success, might find it hard to understand those without such advantages. Economic disparity must not be ignored."[32] While some feminists during the Second Wave began to understand the importance of social class to women's experiences, Second Wave feminism focused more on legal rights for women, leaving socioeconomic issues on the back burner for a time. Today, issues of social class in feminism are apparent as modern feminism continues to struggle to encompass women of all social classes.

The 2013 book *Lean In*, written by feminist and Facebook executive Sheryl Sandberg, exemplified the social class divide in feminism for many. In her book, Sandberg emphasized a kind of individual feminism, urging professional women to "lean in" and take control of their own careers and find power within themselves. But Sandberg focused on equality in the workplace for educated, upper-class women. In her 2014 essay, "Does Feminism Have a Class Problem?" Kathleen Geier asserts that there are structural elements in place keeping women from being as successful as men, no matter how hard they work or how much they "lean in." Geier argues that capitalism and feminism are on a "collision course" because capitalism relies heavily on women's unpaid labor in order to succeed.[33] For example, for someone in a family to work outside of the home, someone else generally must handle the unpaid labor of managing a family and home. Historically, these unpaid household tasks have been the responsibility of women. Geier writes, "It is no accident that that the societies ranked as having the most gender equality are the European social democracies, which tend to have the most economic equality, as well. It is also hardly coincidental that in America over the past twenty years, feminism has stalled while economic inequality has skyrocketed."[34] Overall, there has been a continued reliance on women to provide care for the family, Geier argues.

The feminist movement has struggled to encompass the varied experiences of upper- and lower-class women, most of whom experience discrimination to some degree. Generational differences add to the struggle feminism has in encompassing the experiences of all women. For example, during the Third Wave of feminism, as some feminists made the conscious choice to leave the workforce in order to be stay-at-home

In an effort to be more inclusive, many modern feminists are addressing the needs of mothers. This includes stay-at-home moms and working mothers.

mothers, feminists from previous generations were critical. Feminists from the Second Wave, who had fought so hard to have the right to go to work, struggled to understand a feminist making the decision to stay at home and care for a family. The number of stay-at-home mothers declined to 23 percent in 2000 compared with 49 percent in 1967, but, according to a 2014 study, the number of stay-at-home mothers has steadily been on the rise since 2000. While mothers in low-income families who are unable to afford the cost of childcare make up a portion of this rise in stay-at-home mothers, a quarter of these stay-at-home mothers are college educated.

Some women choose to be stay-at-home moms simply because they want to spend more time with their children. But many, including some college-educated women, essentially are involuntarily becoming stay-at-home moms. Once again, the experiences are diverse. Some mothers say they cannot justify inflexible work hours or expensive childcare. One woman shared her experience in a 2014 news article: "Being laid off from a flexible job and not being able to find a comparable replacement, plus having triplets, plus the cost of daycare for said triplets led me to be a SAHM [stay-at-home-mom]."[35]

Another woman said, "I left a corporate career in public relations following the birth of my oldest because I thought it was important for me to raise my children. Full-time mom became my new career."[36]

> "I left a corporate career in public relations following the birth of my oldest because I thought it was important for me to raise my children. Full-time mom became my new career."[36]
> —A stay-at-home mom

GENERATIONAL DIFFERENCES IN FEMINISM

Another challenge for modern feminism is generational differences, as it can be difficult to unite the different experiences of women of all ages. While generational gaps most certainly exist within feminism, some scholars argue that this is due, at least in part, to a lack of education about what previous movements were about, the women who were a part of them, and what they achieved. The book *Feminism Unfinished* provides an example of this, showing how Second Wave feminists in the twentieth century were unknowingly repeating efforts and important feminist theories from the First Wave feminists a century before. The book states:

*In developing feminist theory [in the late 1960s and early 1970s]
women in consciousness-raising groups were to some extent
reinventing an analysis of women's subordination. Women were
not just ignorant of previous feminist theory—they had been denied
access to it by their education, just as African Americans had been
denied their history. By the end of the nineteenth century, feminists
like Elizabeth Cady Stanton had elaborated a radical, sophisticated
critique of male dominance and, occasionally, of gender itself.*[37]

In this case, feminists were developing theories they thought were new
and starting from scratch when their predecessors had already developed
similar theories. It was just that Second Wave feminists were not aware of
this history. Similarly, modern feminists are often largely unaware of details
about the efforts of feminists who came before them.

THE #METOO MOVEMENT

The #MeToo movement encourages women to speak out against
sexual assault and harassment. The movement focuses on using social
media to show the high number of women who have experienced
sexual harassment or sexual assault. Women post on social media
with the hashtag #MeToo to show they have experienced some level of
harassment or assault. Some include stories of their experiences in their
posts. The hashtag went viral in October 2017, and women all over the
world have been using it to share their stories. Actress Alyssa Milano
is credited with encouraging women to use the hashtag on Twitter to
tell their stories. Many celebrities, including Uma Thurman, Gwyneth
Paltrow, and Jennifer Lawrence, responded. Though Milano is credited
with igniting #MeToo in 2017, the phrase "Me Too" was first used in the
context of sexual harassment awareness in 2006 by activist Tarana
Burke. Milano encouraged the #MeToo hashtag shortly after other women
publicly accused famous Hollywood producer Harvey Weinstein of sexual
assault. Actress Ashley Judd and others said Weinstein had been sexually

TIME'S UP

Growing out of a response to the #MeToo movement and its efforts against sexual harassment and assault against women, the Time's Up movement established a legal defense fund for victims of sexual assault and harassment. A group of Hollywood women launched Time's Up by publishing a letter on January 1, 2018 in the *New York Times*. The letter, which began, "Dear Sisters," stated "We want all survivors of sexual harassment, everywhere, to be heard, to be believed, and to know that accountability is possible." By mid-2018, Time's Up had raised more than $200 million for the legal defense fund. The movement has also gathered more than 200 volunteer lawyers. The focus of Time's Up is to support people who do not have access to the money or media attention that could help them in regard to issues of sexual assault and harassment. The Time's Up website offers victims access to information regarding their rights and a form for applying for the legal defense fund.

Quoted in Time's Up, "Open Letter From Time's Up," The New York Times, *January 1, 2018. www.nytimes.com.*

harassing women for many years. These allegations led to Weinstein's arrest in May 2018.

The #MeToo movement provides a platform and a voice for women who have historically been unable to speak out and be heard on issues of sexual assault and harassment. Even outside of the public allegations on social media using the #MeToo hashtag, the movement has reportedly coincided with some increases in women privately reporting sexual assault and harassment to police. Sexual assault and harassment are known to be underreported crimes, and New York City police officials credited #MeToo with encouraging more women to come forward and report these crimes in late 2017.

But the #MeToo movement is not without controversy. As women are empowered to tell stories of their experiences with sexual harassment, some worry that the men being accused on social media are being judged online without a fair trial in court. In many high-profile cases that have resulted in men resigning or being fired from jobs, the men have admitted to some wrongdoing. Still, the #MeToo movement has sparked debate within the feminist community, even as the movement continues to grow strong. When a writer for *Teen Vogue* tweeted, "Here's an unpopular opinion: I'm actually not at all concerned about innocent men losing their jobs over false assault/harassment accusations," some feminists pointed to a generational divide in the approach to this issue.[38]

> "This [#MeToo] disagreement was quickly characterized in the media as generational. Older feminists, we were told—say, anyone over 40—were sinisterly complicit, laughably outdated, or just too scared of overstepping. Younger women, depending on who you asked, were either righteously passionate, naively idealist, or out for blood."[39]
>
> —*Moira Donegan, writer*

In an essay published in the *Guardian*, Moira Donegan writes about the disagreement that grew within the feminist movement over #MeToo. She writes, "This disagreement was quickly characterized in the media as generational. Older feminists, we were told—say, anyone over 40—were sinisterly complicit, laughably outdated, or just too scared of overstepping. Younger women, depending on who you asked, were either righteously passionate, naively idealist, or out for blood."[39] While Donegan argues that the divide over the #MeToo movement was less about generational gaps and more about different approaches to feminism, many others focused on generational conflict as the #MeToo movement began. In a 2018 essay for the *Chicago Tribune*, author and blogger Courtney Martin, age thirty-eight, shared her perspective: "I have sometimes joked that my generation is feminism's Frankensteins. . . . Our mothers raised us to believe we deserved sexual equality, but now that we're actually demanding it, it can seem overly entitled or sensitive to them."[40]

ROE V. WADE

Roe v. Wade was the landmark decision of the Supreme Court in 1973 stating that it was unconstitutional for states to criminalize abortions. The court ruled that the right to privacy under the Fourteenth Amendment extended to a woman's right to decide to have a child. The court argued that this right should be balanced with the state's rights to regulate abortion; therefore, abortions were allowed to be regulated during the third trimester. This meant that an abortion could be legal as long as the fetus was not viable, though viability may vary from case to case. This decision was affirmed in the 1992 case *Planned Parenthood v. Casey*. *Roe v. Wade* sparked a national debate that continues until today, and there are protests and movements on both sides of the pro-life and pro-choice debates. In recent years, states have taken measures to roll back abortion rights, challenging the 1973 decision. A 2014 Gallup poll showed that 50 percent of Americans believe that abortion should be legal in certain circumstances, 28 percent believe abortion should be legal under any circumstances, and 21 percent believe that abortion should be illegal, no matter the circumstance.

THE PRO-LIFE AND PRO-CHOICE DEBATE

But generational differences are just one of many obstacles modern feminism faces. It is difficult to unite all women when their goals of a feminist movement vary. One such example of this is the pro-life and pro-choice abortion debate that exists within modern feminism. Those who are pro-life believe abortion should be illegal, but those who are pro-choice believe that abortion should be a legal choice for women. Because many feminists see this issue as central to the feminist movement, differing perspectives on this issue can make unification next to impossible for some feminists. Historically, feminist movements have been closely connected with pro-choice efforts, but many feminists are pro-life.

On one side of the issue, US Rep. Carolyn Maloney of New York wrote in 2008 about her concerns related to the limitations now being set on legal abortions throughout the United States. She wrote:

We haven't regressed all the way back to the mid-'60s, but we're getting dangerously close. . . . Reproductive rights have experienced the worst backsliding in recent years. Things today are far worse than they were in the wake of Roe v. Wade *in 1973. Reproductive health care that allows women to manage their own fertility and saves and improves women's lives is under assault by a well-organized, well-financed, anti-choice movement that extends all the way to the White House.*[41]

While access to safe and legal abortions remains an important issue for many feminists, there are other feminists who are against abortion and argue for better support for women who have children. Helen Alvaré, a law professor at George Mason University, has written about the large number of pro-life feminists. She contends that many women are feminists but may avoid the label *feminist* because it is often associated with the pro-choice movement. She argues that there are many women working hard for women's rights who are part of the pro-life movement. She writes:

They [pro-life feminists] know, live and openly articulate women's essential equality and dignity, and women's rights to the same opportunities afforded men. They want these opportunities not only for themselves, but also for their daughters, sisters, and friends. At the very same time, they recoil at the thought of abortion. Not because they are judging the women involved, but because—as even Justices John Paul Stevens and Ruth Bader Ginsburg have observed in their abortion opinions—abortion can be "gruesome" and "brutal."[42]

Pro-choice feminists argue that making abortions illegal will not stop abortions, as history has shown that women with unwanted pregnancies will often find unsafe ways to end their pregnancies. But the issue is certainly a complex one for modern feminists to contend with and explore. Time will tell if feminists who disagree on abortion will be able to work together for women's rights.

Senator Tammy Duckworth, a Democrat from Illinois, is one of the 107 women serving in US Congress as of early 2018. Duckworth lost her legs fighting in the Iraq War (2003–2011) and has spoken out on issues related to veterans.

GOVERNMENT REPRESENTATION

Another obstacle that modern feminism faces is the lack of female representation in the US government. In the 2010 census, women made up 50.8 percent of the US population, yet in 2018, they made up only 20 percent of the United States Congress. There are twenty-three women out of 100 senators and eighty-four women out of the 435 members

WOMEN IN THE
US CONGRESS, 2018

■ **WOMEN**

■ **MEN**

23

84

SENATE
100 MEMBERS

HOUSE OF
REPRESENTATIVES
435 MEMBERS

While women make up approximately half of the United States population, they are not represented that way in federal government. As of July 2018, there were 107 women serving in Congress. Twenty-three of the country's 100 senators were women, and eighty-four of the 435 members of the House of Representatives were women. This unequal representation persists at lower levels of government. At the state level, only six of the country's fifty governors were women.

"Women in the U.S. Congress 2018," Center For American Women and Politics, *n.d. www.cawp.rutgers.edu.*

of the House of Representatives. The United States ranks 104th in the world when it comes to women representation in government, falling from fifty-second just two decades ago as a result of advancements for women in terms of government representation in other countries. Some countries have passed laws requiring a balance in male and female representation in the government. Authors Soo Oh and Sarah Kliff describe the significance of the United States' low ranking for women in government. In addition to lack of political representation for women, the low number of female government leaders makes it harder for young women and girls to see government leadership positions as a possibility for their futures. According to Oh and Kliff, recent research "shows that women consistently co-sponsor more bills related to women's health than their male counterparts, regardless of liberal or conservative ideology. But more importantly, having more women in government changes how society thinks about all women—and how young women think about themselves."[43]

Despite the United States' struggle with equal representation in government, there are still several female government leaders who are working to make a big difference in the lives of women, children, and all families. Elizabeth Warren, a Democratic senator from Massachusetts, is one of the most notable and outspoken progressives in Congress. She is known for fighting for the rights of average Americans over the needs of big businesses, and she has made an important name for herself in her fight for issues such as government oversight of financial institutions and health care for all Americans. Elected in 2012, Warren was the first female senator from Massachusetts. Another high-profile woman in government is Tammy Duckworth, a Democratic senator from Illinois. She was elected to the Senate in 2016 after serving in the House of Representatives from 2013 to 2017. Before she became a politician, Duckworth served as an Army helicopter pilot in the Iraq War (2003–2011), which caused her to lose her legs as a result of injuries. She has spoken out on supporting

Democrat Hillary Clinton, former secretary of state and former first lady, was the first woman nominated for president by a major political party. While Clinton lost the 2016 election to Republican Donald Trump, an increased number of women have run for political office since then.

veterans, fighting homelessness, and other issues. She also is the first senator to give birth while in office. Tammy Baldwin, a senator from Wisconsin, is the first openly-gay person elected to the US Senate and has fought for national health care reform as well as issues related specifically to women's health care. There are also important female leaders currently serving on the Supreme Court—Ruth Bader Ginsburg,

Sonia Sotomayor, and Elena Kagan. Of the 113 Supreme Court justices throughout history, just four of them have been women.

Women in the United States are organizing and moving into the future in an effort to improve the lives of all women. Since the 2016 presidential election—in which Hillary Clinton, the first woman nominated for president by a major political party, lost to Donald Trump—more women are running for political office than ever before. While women running for office still face many challenges, a record number of women ran for Congress in the 2018 midterm elections. At the end of April 2018, 527 women were running for these offices, a jump of 67 percent from 2016.

CHAPTER FOUR

WHAT IS THE FUTURE OF FEMINISM?

As feminists continue to work toward a future of gender equality, modern feminism will continue evolving. Many are working to make the movement more intersectional and inclusive of all women. Additionally, feminists continue grappling with the movement's public image.

Modern feminists are being met with some public misrepresentation of what feminism is, including perpetuation of negative stereotypes.

In her journal article "The 'F' Word: How the Media Frame Feminism," educator and scholar Debra Baker Beck wrote, "The mainstream media can seldom be accused of being friendly to feminism. In fact, many of the challenges the women's movement faces can be traced to the way various media—

> "The mainstream media can seldom be accused of being friendly to feminism. In fact, many of the challenges the women's movement faces can be traced to the way various media—broadcast, print, and film—portray the movement and the issues it has tried to address."[44]
> —Debra Baker Beck, educator and scholar

EMMA WATSON'S UNITED NATIONS SPEECH

Emma Watson is a British actress known for her role in the *Harry Potter* films. She has used her celebrity status to campaign for gender equality. She is a United Nations Goodwill ambassador, and she made headlines in 2014 when she launched the HeForShe initiative. In September 2014, she gave a speech at the United Nations headquarters in New York City. Her speech has become famous for its eloquent advocacy for equality for women. In her speech, she described how some in the media treated her in a sexualized way at age fourteen. She argued in favor of feminism and the term *feminism*. She said, "I decided that I was a feminist, and this seemed uncomplicated to me. But my recent research has shown me that feminism has become an unpopular word. Women are choosing not to identify as feminists. Apparently, I'm among the ranks of women whose expressions are seen as too strong, too aggressive, isolating, and anti-men. Unattractive even." Watson goes on to explain the need for feminism, and her speech has inspired many women, especially women of her generation.

Emma Watson, "HeForShe Speech," UN Women, September 20, 2014.
www.unwomen.org.

broadcast, print, and film—portray the movement and the issues it has tried to address."[44]

There are efforts to end both the confusion about what feminism is and the negative stereotypes associated with it. Moving to the future, many young Americans, both men and women, are organizing and making even greater efforts to equate women's rights with human rights. Actress Emma Watson, famous for her role in the *Harry Potter* movies, inspires many young feminists and appears to be one of many young leaders of feminism as feminism moves into the future. In a 2014 speech at the United Nations headquarters in New York City, Watson called for a better understanding of the term *feminism* and dismissed the negative stereotypes associated with it. She also argued for a new understanding of gender, to show that gender is not always the same as biological sex and that it can be many things on a fluid spectrum rather than just male or female. In her speech, Watson said, "Both men and women should feel free to be sensitive. Both men and women should feel free to be strong. It is time that we all perceive gender on a spectrum, instead of two sets of opposing ideals. If we stop defining each other by what we are not, and start defining ourselves by who we are, we can all be freer."[45] For many, this openness on gender and inclusivity of all men and women is what the future of feminism looks like.

LESSONS FROM THE WOMEN'S MARCH ON WASHINGTON

The Women's March on Washington was one of the most important events in the modern feminist movement, and it has revealed important lessons about the future of feminism. When the march was criticized for being too narrow in its definition of women's experiences, organizers responded with materials of inclusivity and a mission statement to make it clear that this generation of women would be working to consider a wide range of voices. After the Women's March, many prominent black feminists spoke out against joining with white women to protest. They said many of these white women had remained silent for the Black Lives Matter movement and for protests against the Dakota Access oil pipeline's potential dangers to the Standing Rock Sioux Indian Reservation.

The Women's March group responded with renewed efforts toward intersectionality in feminism, and it appointed black feminist Tamika Mallory as cochair of the organization. According to Mallory, "I think there were a lot of black women who said, 'I did my job, and now that (you're) woke and it's personal for you and you want to have a march, that's awesome. And now I'm expecting you to meet me on the battlefield.' That's where the real work will begin. And so the skepticism can be not so much corrected, but it can be challenged by white women showing up literally every day after the march."[46]

A second Women's March in 2018, on the anniversary of President Trump's inauguration, showed that there was still high energy in the movement. Although the follow-up march did not have a historic number of participants like the first march, the 2018 march in New York City alone spanned twenty city blocks. And the focus of the march was on more inclusivity, proving that the Women's March organization could grow and change in order to meet the needs of more women. Bob Bland, a woman who cofounded the march, said, "We learned about the history and the ways we were causing harm and trauma to communities of color, and we centered women of color in leadership and became intentional as white women about holding space."[47]

"I think there were a lot of black women who said, 'I did my job, and now that (you're) woke and it's personal for you and you want to have a march, that's awesome. And now I'm expecting you to meet me on the battlefield.' That's where the real work will begin. And so the skepticism can be not so much corrected, but it can be challenged by white women showing up literally every day after the march."[46]
—Tamika Mallory, Women's March cochair

THE NEED FOR MORE INTERSECTIONAL FEMINISM

Despite the fact that many prominent feminists have been women of color throughout the history of feminism, from Sojourner Truth to bell hooks, the feminist movement as a whole has been criticized for focusing too much on the experiences of white, middle-class women. Because these women were often the ones most able to protest and speak out, their voices have been the loudest. But educational efforts within the feminist movement are helping white women better understand the perspectives of women of color. Women of color and women in the LGBTQIA community are also finding ways to embrace feminism despite generally feeling left out of the movement historically. Some are spearheading branches of feminism specific to their own experiences. Author Gayle Pitman explains:

Some people say modern feminism still needs to be more intersectional. This would include better representation of women of color, members of the LGBTQIA community, and low-income women, among others.

Despite the oppression women have experienced within mainstream feminism, women have found many ways to insert themselves into the movement. Some have fought to create a place at the table alongside White women. Others have created their own branches of feminism. Womanism, for example, focuses on the experiences of African-American women. Mujeristas are Latina feminists, who address issues like immigration, religion, and family, as well as gender roles. Queer and trans feminism . . . takes up the needs of sexual and gender minorities. All of these approaches involve taking an intersectional approach to feminism.[48]

ISSUES UNITING WOMEN

Despite the obstacles that modern feminism faces, it still appears that recent social issues in the United States are starting to bring all women together in a way that has not been seen in recent history. These issues deal with women's rights, rights for people of color, immigrant rights, children's rights, and environmental issues. Currently, the United States struggles compared with the rest of the industrialized world in issues related to health care, socioeconomic status, and human rights. Many people feel that issues they believe in are being threatened on many fronts. This is partly because of 2017 and 2018 legislation proposed in the United States that limits women's access to reproductive care and enacts policies regarding the US-Mexico border that many throughout the world consider to be human rights violations. As such, many women and men are working together to form a resistance movement in the United States. Protests continue throughout the country through marches, publications, and efforts on social media.

While motherhood as a feminist issue remains an unpopular topic among many scholars in formal feminist theory, it is an important topic in feminist blogs and social media. The internet is giving voices to many feminist moms. Women are writing about raising feminist daughters and sons and networking via blogs and social media. Many feminist moms are taking to the internet to share their stories and empower other moms. Feminist "mommy bloggers" have become so popular that *Ms.* magazine and other major women's publications are working to introduce these blogs to their readers. Blogs such as *Viva La Feminista*, *Blue Milk*, and *Undercover in the Suburbs* are connecting feminist moms and exploring issues important to the women's rights movement. Part of the goal of feminist mom bloggers is to empower other women and explore issues related to raising children as a feminist. Sarah Cottrell, creator of the *Housewife Plus* blog, wrote about how parents can raise children who care about equality in our culture. She writes:

"Don't just teach [children] that pink and blue are not a competing faction, also teach them that true equality—true feminism—is about equal access for everyone. All people need access to medicine, food, protection, education, shelter, and safety. . . . No matter how different people are, everyone deserves to be treated with compassion, respect, and the same rights."[49]

—Sarah Cottrell, Housewife Plus blogger

Don't just teach them that pink and blue are not a competing faction, also teach them that true equality—true feminism—is about equal access for everyone. All people need access to medicine, food, protection, education, shelter, and safety. . . . No matter how different people are, everyone deserves to be treated with compassion, respect, and the same rights. It's also essential to discuss white privilege: what it means, how it affects society, and how we must work to dismantle systemic racism so that our democracy and justice system isn't oppressing people of color.[49]

CHANGING THE FACE OF MOTHERHOOD

Motherhood is changing, and, as such, future generations will be changed. Feminist moms are understanding the importance of raising boys to not only respect women but also to be free of the patriarchal expectations of men that can inhibit boys. For example, more mothers are understanding the importance of teaching boys that it is all right to cry, as there are clear connections between expressing emotions and good mental health. But men are also sharing more of the workload when it comes to parenting. As more women are becoming the breadwinners in many American families, stay-at-home dads are also becoming more common. In 2012, the number of stay-at-home dads in America was estimated to be 2 million, up from 1.1 million in 1989. According to a 2016 report from the Center for American Progress, 42 percent of mothers were the "sole or primary family breadwinners" in 2015.[50] Black and Latina women were more likely to be a family's sole breadwinner, but the numbers are on the rise among white women as well. While the reasons for the rise in stay-at-home dads in America are varied and complex, the overall shift in terms of who stays at home with children and who works outside the home ultimately has an effect on American culture.

However, because women's pay lags behind men's, these numbers are not necessarily the positive outcome that many feminists would hope to see. There is a connection between the rise in women breadwinners and the rise in poverty in American families, and the numbers are getting worse, leading many feminists to reignite issues surrounding equal pay. Premilla Nadasen, author and professor at Barnard College, writes:

> The growth of extreme poverty in the land of plenty is an indicator that we shouldn't be talking about how to slash spending on social programs, but how to expand services and better meet the needs of the vulnerable among us. One and a half million American households live in extreme poverty today, nearly twice as many as 20 years ago. If this trend continues, we will undoubtedly see the number of extremely poor Americans rise dramatically, imperiling the values of democracy and human rights.[51]

This issue remains a challenge for feminism going forward, and some women in government are working to raise more awareness to the ways that the gender pay gap affects families. In her book *Rumors of Our Progress Have Been Greatly Exaggerated*, Congresswoman Carolyn B. Maloney writes about her experiences working to help women with children: "Wanting to help people who really needed my help, I got a job working with welfare recipients who were trying to get their high school equivalency degrees in East Harlem. The women I worked with faced terrible decisions every day: diapers or milk, dinner or rent, go deeper into debt or postpone Christmas until next year."[52] Family poverty has long been a concern of feminism, and with this issue on the rise, chances are that this is an issue feminism will need to continue to address.

Working women generally make less money than their male counterparts. This pay gap can be stressful for any woman, but some experts have highlighted working mothers as being particularly affected.

Many women are calling for government intervention to aid in women's rights and issues of unequal pay. The United States remains the only developed country in the world not to offer paid maternity leave for mothers. Moreover, according to the United Nations, out of 170 countries studied in 2016, the United States and New Guinea were the only countries not to offer some kind of government-mandated paid maternity leave. There are just 195 countries in the world. This means many American women have to choose between staying at home with their children and supporting their families. According to a 2018 report from the Washington Center for Equitable Growth, more than 70 percent of families rely on the mother's income, but moms who work in full-time positions make just 71 percent of what full-time working dads make. The connections between poverty and the health of women and children

FIFTH WAVE FEMINISM

Feminist scholars often note the lack of a clear gap between the Third Wave and Fourth Wave of feminism. It was as if the Fourth Wave grew organically out of the Third Wave, expanding on lessons of intersectionality from the Third Wave and organizing activism via the internet and social media. Similarly, a Fifth Wave of feminism may be growing organically out of the Fourth Wave of feminism. While the Fifth Wave is far from developed, some feminists are now calling for this new wave of the movement. Author and feminist Caitlin Moran calls for a Fifth Wave of feminism in her book, a feminist manifesto entitled *How to Be a Woman*, published in 2011. In the book, she calls for a new kind of feminism that embraces being a woman and uses humor to deal with the awkwardness and struggles of being a modern woman in western culture. Moran also calls for a fight against the damage that patriarchy does to women and contends that all women should be feminists.

make financial issues one of the biggest concerns feminism must face in the coming years.

Feminists are also organizing to address many other issues, including health care access, gun violence, and environmental conservation. The lack of equal representation of women in government can make it difficult for women's voices to be heard on these issues, but feminists are not giving up. Women have created blogs and organized protests using social media. Some feminists are angry, not at men, but at a system that oppresses women, children, and even men, and they are increasingly calling for action and protest against the patriarchal system. Lessa Leigh, intersectional feminist activist and cofounder of the blog *Feminactivist*, writes about the need for activism. In a 2018 post, she wrote:

What can we do to change course? For our survival, we have to start thinking about radical forms of engagement and civil disobedience. Thoughts and prayers are no longer enough (were they ever?). We will need to devise ways of sharing information and communicating that are as secure as possible. We will need to disrupt the system in any way possible: protesting, boycotting, bartering, voting (and how ironic that voting could be considered "radical", but here we are), educating, sabotaging, infiltrating, and distracting while simultaneously using whatever parts of the system work to our advantage.[53]

Ultimately, the future of feminism in America will be revealed in the way American women and men find ways to resist the patriarchal structure of society and understand the importance of equality for everyone, regardless of gender, race, or ability. This will be reflected in how people raise their children to understand the importance of equality. As feminist Chimamanda Ngozi Adichie says, "Gender matters everywhere in the world. And I would like today to ask that we should begin to dream about and plan for a different world. A fairer world. A world of happier men and happier women who are truer to themselves. And this is how we start: we must raise our daughters differently. We must also raise our sons differently."[54]

> "Gender matters everywhere in the world. And I would like today to ask that we should begin to dream about and plan for a different world. A fairer world. A world of happier men and happier women who are truer to themselves. And this is how we start: we must raise our daughters differently. We must also raise our sons differently."[54]
> —*Chimamanda Ngozi Adichie, writer*

In future generations, what will feminism look like? While feminism will likely continue to face struggles with its image and with inclusivity, progress is being made, progress toward a broader definition of feminism. Feminists are making progress toward a movement that includes women of all backgrounds and addresses all forms of oppression. In her 2017 article "What Does a Feminist Future Look Like?" Lorna O'Hara wrote:

Feminism is experiencing a clear resurgence in popularity. In fact, a friend of mine recently told me that [retail store] H&M is even selling t-shirts that say "Feminist" on them . . . Something is definitely happening. In fact, some claim that we're in a "fourth wave" of

Some longtime feminist activists say that feminism and activism have surged in popularity since the 2016 election of President Trump. They say they hope the motivation for activism continues into the future.

feminism, one which aims to put into practice the inclusivity and intersectionality proposed in the third wave and which distinguishes itself by the use of new technologies, particularly the internet and social media.[55]

Feminism has been an important part of America's history, and it is changing and evolving to meet the needs of the twenty-first century. Activism seems to be growing and changing as each new generation recreates feminism to fit its needs. And some say recent political events, such as the election of President Trump in 2016, may be making feminism more important than ever. Modern feminists are growing the movement into one that is likely to continue on into the future. In a 2018 interview, iconic feminist Gloria Steinem said, "I've never seen this much activism in my life. . . . It's way, way more than anything I've ever seen."[56]

SOURCE NOTES

INTRODUCTION: FEMINISM TODAY

1. Chimamanda Ngozi Adichie, *We Should All Be Feminists.* New York: Anchor Books, 2015, p. 48.

2. Julia Bluhm, "9 Reasons Why We Need Feminism More Now Than Ever," *The Lala,* August 19, 2017. www.thelala.com.

CHAPTER 1: WHAT IS THE HISTORY BEHIND FEMINISM?

3. Raj Patel and Jason W. Moore, "How the Chicken Nugget Became the True Symbol of Our Era," *The Guardian,* May 8, 2018. www.theguardian.com.

4. Sheila Rowbotham, *Hidden from History: 300 Years of Women's Oppression and the Fight Against It.* London, United Kingdom: Pluto Press, 1977, p. 5.

5. Christopher L.C.E. Witcombe, "Eve's Identity," *Eve and the Identity of Women,* 2000. www.arthistoryresources.net.

6. Sally Roesch-Wagner, "The Untold Story of Iroquois Influence on Early Feminists," *Feminist.com,* 1996. www.feminist.com.

7. Una A. Robertson, *The Illustrated History of the Housewife, 1650-1950.* New York: St. Martin's Press, 1999.

8. Roesch-Wagner, "The Untold Story of Iroquois Influence on Early Feminists."

9. Abigail Adams, "Letter to John Adams," *National Archives,* March 31, 1776. founders.archives.gov.

10. Harvard Business School, "Women at Work: Manual Labor," *Women, Enterprise, & Society,* 2010. www.library.hbs.edu.

11. Margaret Fuller, *Woman in the Nineteenth Century.* Salt Lake City, Utah: Project Gutenberg, August 2012. www.gutenberg.org.

12. Jean V. Matthews, *Women's Struggle for Equality: The First Phase, 1828-1897.* Chicago, Illinois: Ivan R. Dee, 1997. p. 59.

13. Matthews, *Women's Struggle for Equality,* p. 110.

14. Matthews, *Women's Struggle for Equality*, pp. 111–112.

15. Carolyn B. Maloney, *Rumors of Our Progress Have Been Greatly Exaggerated*. Emmaus, Pennsylvania: Modern Times, 2008. p. 165.

CHAPTER 2: WHAT DOES MODERN FEMINISM LOOK LIKE?

16. Rebecca Walker, "Becoming the Third Wave," *Ms.*, January 1992. www.msmagazine.com.

17. bell hooks, *Feminism Is for Everybody*. New York: Routledge, 2015.

18. "Feminist Theory and Criticism," *Encyclopedia of African-American Culture and History*, 2006. www.encyclopedia.com.

19. Janet Lee and Susan M. Shaw, *Women's Voices Feminist Visions*. New York: McGraw Hill, 2015. p. 15.

20. Alia E. Dastagir, "What Is Intersectional Feminism? A Look at the Term You May Be Hearing A Lot." *USA Today*, January 19, 2017. www.usatoday.com.

21. Quoted in Constance Grady, "The Waves of Feminism, and Why People Keep Fighting Over Them, Explained," *Vox*, July 20, 2018. www.vox.com.

22. Martha Rampton, "Four Waves of Feminism," *Pacific University Magazine*, 2008. magazine.pacificu.edu.

23. Emily Peck, "One-Quarter of Mothers Return to Work Less Than Two Weeks After Giving Birth, Report Finds," *Huffington Post,* August 8, 2015. www.huffingtonpost.com.

24. Gayle E. Pitman, *Feminism from A to Z*. Washington D.C.: Magination Press, 2017. p. 105.

25. Pitman, *Feminism from A to Z*, p. 110.

26. Katha Pollitt, "Actually, Not Everything Is a Feminist Issue," *Nation*, March 23, 2017. www.thenation.com.

27. "Our Mission," *Women's March*, n.d., www.womensmarch.com.

28. "Our Mission."

CHAPTER 3: WHAT OBSTACLES DOES MODERN FEMINISM FACE?

29. Elizabeth Johnston, "The Original 'Nasty Woman,'" *Atlantic*, November 6, 2016. www.theatlantic.com.

30. Carmen Rios, "If We Divide, We Don't Conquer: 3 Reasons Why Feminists Need to Talk About Race," *Everyday Feminism*, February 1, 2015. www.everydayfeminism.com.

31. T.S. Holloway, "Why This Black Girl Will Not Be Returning to the Women's March," *Huffington Post,* January 19, 2018. www.huffingtonpost.com.

32. Dorothy Sue Cobble, Linda Gordon, and Astrid Henry, *Feminism Unfinished: A Short Surprising History of American Women's Movements*. New York: Liveright Publishing Corporation, 2014, p. 63–64.

33. Kathleen Geier, "Does Feminism Have a Class Problem?" *Nation*, June 11, 2014. www.thenation.com.

34. Geier, "Does Feminism Have a Class Problem?"

35. Quoted in Kavita Varma-White, "10 Moms Tell Us Why They Chose Home Over Work," *Today*, April 8, 2014. www.today.com.

36. Quoted in Varma-White, "10 Moms Tell Us Why They Chose Home Over Work."

37. Cobble, Gordon, and Henry, *Feminism Unfinished*, p. 84.

38. Emily Lindin, *Twitter*, November 21, 2017. www.twitter.com.

39. Moira Donegan, "How #MeToo Revealed the Central Rift Within Feminism Today," *The Guardian*, May 11, 2018. www.theguardian.com.

40. David Crary and Tamara Lush, "#MeToo Movement Starting to Show Generational Divides," *Chicago Tribune*, January 29, 2018. www.chicagotribune.com.

41. Maloney, *Rumors of Our Progress Have Been Greatly Exaggerated*, p. 166.

42. Helen Alvaré, "Open Your Eyes, Pro-Life Feminists Are Everywhere," *CNN*, May 23, 2018. www.cnn.com.

43. Soo Oh and Sarah Kliff, "The U.S. Is Ranked 104th in Women's Representation in Government," *Vox*, March 8, 2017. www.vox.com.

CHAPTER 4: WHAT IS THE FUTURE OF FEMINISM?

44. Debra Baker Beck, "The 'F' Word: How the Media Frame Feminism." *NWSA Journal*, March 1998, pp. 139–153.

45. Quoted in Nicki Lisa Cole, "Emma Watson's 2014 Speech on Gender Equality," *ThoughtCo*, June 1, 2018. www.thoughtco.com.

46. Quoted in Ashley Stoney, "The Woman Driving Inclusion at the Women's March on Washington," *Huffington Post*, March 31, 2017. www.huffingtonpost.com.

47. Emma Gray, Alana Vagianos, and Laura Bassett, "Nevertheless, She Persisted: A Year After the First Women's March, Energy Is Still High." *Huffington Post*, January 20, 2018. www.huffingtonpost.com.

48. Pitman, *Feminism from A to Z*, p. 69.

49. Sarah Cottrell, "How To Raise Forward-Thinking Children." *Scary Mommy*, n.d. www.scarymommy.com.

50. Quoted in Samantha Cooney, "More Women Are Their Family's Sole Breadwinner Than Ever Before," *Time*, December 20, 2016. www.time.com.

51. Premilla Nadasen, "Extreme Poverty Returns to America," *Washington Post*, December 21, 2017. www.washingtonpost.com.

52. Maloney, *Rumors of Our Progress Have Been Greatly Exaggerated*, p. xii.

53. Lessa Leigh, "Saving America from Itself," *Feminactivist*, June 25, 2018. feminactivist.wordpress.com.

54. Adichie, *We Should All Be Feminists*, p. 25.

55. Lorna O'Hara, "What Does a Feminist Future Look Like?," *Huffington Post*, November 30, 2017. www.huffingtonpost.com.

56. Quoted in Alanna Vagianos, "Gloria Steinhem: 'I've Never Seen This Much Activism in My Life,'" *Huffington Post*, May 7, 2018. www.huffingtonpost.com.

FOR FURTHER RESEARCH

BOOKS

Chimamanda Ngozi Adichie, *We Should All Be Feminists*. New York: Anchor Books, 2015.

Dorothy Sue Cobble, Linda Gordon, and Astrid Henry, *Feminism Unfinished: A Short Surprising History of American Women's Movements*. New York: Liveright Publishing Corporation, 2014.

bell hooks, *Feminism Is for Everybody: Passionate Politics*. New York: Routledge, 2015.

Carolyn B. Maloney, *Rumors of Our Progress Have Been Greatly Exaggerated*. Emmaus, PA: Modern Times, 2008.

INTERNET SOURCES

Rosemary Counter, "Caitlin Moran Forces Us to Ask, Is It Time For Fifth-Wave Feminism?" *Globe and Mail*, August 17, 2012. www.theglobeandmail.com.

Alia E. Dastagir, "What Is Intersectional Feminism? A Look At the Term You May Be Hearing A Lot," *USA Today*, January 19, 2017. www.usatoday.com.

Kathleen Geier, "Does Feminism Have a Class Problem?" *Nation*, June 11, 2014. www.thenation.com.

S. T. Holloway, "Why This Black Girl Will Not Be Returning to the Women's March," *Huffington Post*, January 19, 2018. www.huffingtonpost.com.

Elizabeth Johnston, "The Original 'Nasty Woman,'" *Atlantic*, November 6, 2016. www.theatlantic.com.

Martha Rampton, "Four Waves of Feminism," *Pacific University Magazine*, 2008. magazine.pacificu.edu.

WEBSITES

Feminist.com
www.feminist.com

This site provides an online community and a wide variety of resources on feminism. It is a nonprofit organization.

Institute for Women's Policy Research
www.iwpr.org

The Institute for Women's Policy Research is an organization that shares research and information in order to help improve the lives of women from all backgrounds. The organization works to advance women's statuses through social science research, policy analysis, and public education.

The Women's March
www.womensmarch.com

This site offers resources related to the Women's March on Washington in 2017, explains the organization's mission, and works to empower women.

INDEX

IMAGE CREDITS

Cover: © Jacob Lund/Shutterstock Images

4: © National Woman's Party records/Library of Congress

5: © Shala W. Graham/Shutterstock Images

8: © Shala W. Graham/Shutterstock Images

11: © Jorisvo/iStockphoto

16: © Everett - Art/Shutterstock Images

18: © Ann Rosener/Farm Security Administration/Office of War Information Photograph Collection/Library of Congress

21: © National Woman's Party records/Library of Congress

31: © arindambanerjee/Shutterstock Images

33: © ucchie79/Shutterstock Images

36: © Jose Luis Magana/AP Images

38: © SpeedKingz/Shutterstock Images

41: © Shelli Jensen/Shutterstock Images

44: © Jim Lambert/Shutterstock Images

46: © NinaViktoria/Shutterstock Images

53: © Gregory Reed/Shutterstock Images

54: © Red Line Editorial

56: © Evan El-Amin/Shutterstock Images

62: © Rainmaker Photo/MediaPunch/Ipx/AP Images

66: © kurhan/Shutterstock Images

69: © Houdek Martina/CTK/AP Images

ABOUT THE **AUTHOR**

Crystal Sands is a writing professor and freelance writer. She has published several reference books and dozens of reference articles. She has two sons and lives on a Maine homestead with her husband where they work together to raise a family, chickens, and a garden.